Gary Jones

Helsinki

First published by Gary Jones in 2017

Copyright © Gary Jones, 2017

All rights reserved. No part of this publication may be reproduced, stored, or transmitted in any form or by any means, electronic, mechanical, photocopying, recording, scanning, or otherwise without written permission from the publisher. It is illegal to copy this book, post it to a website, or distribute it by any other means without permission.

This book was professionally typeset on Reedsy.
Find out more at reedsy.com

Contents

Introduction	1
Helsinki Then & Now	4
When Is the Best Time to Visit Helsinki?	10
What You Need to Know about Transportation	14
HOTELS :Best Affordable & Quality Hotels	27
Let's Eat: Best Restaurants in Helsinki	33
Exploring The Legendary Landmarks in Helsinki	38
It's Museum Time: Best Museums in Helsinki	49
Appreciation for the Arts: Top 5 Art Galleries	57
The Best-Tasting Coffee: Top 5 Coffee Shops	62
Exploring the Bars in Helsinki: Top 5 Bars	66
How to Enjoy a Night in Helsinki: Top 5 Night Clubs	69
Only in Helsinki: The Special Things that You Can Do in the City	73
Mind Your Safety	77
Experiencing Helsinki: A 3-Day Travel Itinerary	81
Conclusion	90

1

Introduction

So You're Going to **Helsinki?**

"Tervetuloa"

That's the Finnish translation of the English word "welcome."

Once you step foot in Helsinki, Finland's capital city, that's a word you'll probably hear often. Since the Finns are typically accommodating and hospitable, having an awkward introductory experience is unlikely. They'll shake your hand, and they might even ask you whether you want them to show you around.

There, a glorious batch of interesting people, historical landmarks, one-of-a-kind attractions, unique traditions, art galleries, nightclubs, and other exciting things are waiting for you!

If you're after an outrageous journey, it's the ideal place for you. So why not check it out?

Make sure to have enough money (in euros) with you. Have plans in place and you're good to go!

INTRODUCTION

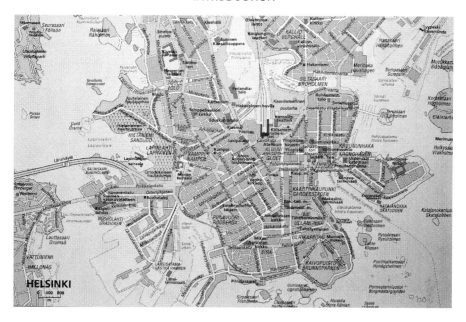

2

Helsinki Then & Now

When you approach a local in Helsinki about your location, don't be surprised if he tells you "you're in this (___) part of Hessa" or "you're in this part of Stadi".

You might freak out for a bit. But, learn to keep it cool. You're still in Helsinki.

The slang words for Helsinki are Hessa and Stadi. Many locals use these informal terms frequently.

Moreover, the words Hessa and Stadi are but two in the lineup of uncommon things about the capital city. Because Helsinki has been an (unofficial) residence since the 14th century, it's very rich in history. Definitely, there's still plenty of information about it worth discovering.

A Brief History
The founder of Helsinki is Sweden's King Gustavus Vasa. He founded the Russian-dependent city on December 6, 1550. It began with the reputation as the competitor city of Estonia's Tallinn and as Southern Finland's new trading port.

In 1812, Helsinki was recognized officially as a progressive city. It was also then that Helsinki became Finland's capital.

From then on, developments began. It soon became an industrial and an administrative place. It started to make way for economic and political growth.

Facts about the city during the early days:
- Helsinki had a strong reputation. Despite the unforgettable marks

of the Finnish Winter War and the Finnish Civil War, it thrived.
- The original city name is Helsingfors (in Swedish) and Gelsingfors (in Russian).
- To reduce the Swedish influence on Helsinki's people, The Royal Academy of Turku (Russia's 1st university), was relocated to Finland's capital city.

Location, Population & Geography
-Helsinki is located in the southern part of Finland, on the Gulf of Finland's shore and in the Uusimaa region. To the east is Stockholm, Sweden (400 km). To the west is Saint Petersburg, Russia (388 km). To the North is Tallinn, Estonia (80 km).

As of 2016, Helsinki has a city population of more than 600,000 and an urban population of more than 1,100,000. The city has a majority of bilingual speakers since Finland is officially bilingual. 84% of the population speaks Finnish, 6% speaks Swedish, and the remaining 10% speaks a mix of English and other languages.

Daughter of the Baltic is Helsinki's other name. The particular name acknowledges its location at the peninsula's tip. It's surrounded by more than 300 islands. The major islands are Korkeasaari, Lauttasaari, Seurasaari, and Vallisaari.

The Capital Region & the Metropolis

Helsinki's Capital Region consists of four municipalities. These municipalities are Espoo, Helsinki, Kaunianen, and Vantaa. It has a high housing density since 0.2% of its surface area is allotted for 20% of Finland's total population.

Meanwhile, Helsinki's Metropolitan Area (or the Greater Helsinki region) is the northernmost area in the world. It consists of 11 surrounding municipalities. It covers an area of more than 3, 600 km2. As of 2016, you can find an estimation of ¼ of Finland's total population in the Metropolitan Area.

Maintaining a 1st Class Reputation

In 1995, when Finland became a part of the European Union, growth was achieved. Helsinki was recognized as a center for educational, financial, economic, and political affairs. As of 2016, more than 70% of major companies operating in Finland are located in the capital city.

Helsinki has continued to progress through the years. Because of its impressive reputation, it has garnered major recognitions. Two of these are: (1) it was included in the Livable Cities Index 2011, according to Monocle and (2) it was in the top 10 of the best cities worldwide, according to the Economist's Intelligence Unit.

3

When Is the Best Time to Visit Helsinki?

There's this phenomenon called The Midnight Sun.

It's a natural occurrence during the summer solstice. It shows the sun's availability during midnight. Because of its splendid sight, it offers a relaxing view.

Astronomers of all levels and travelers are among the bunch who call themselves fans of the natural phenomenon. You might want to be one of them, too. After all, you might not get to see the sun during midnight.

Where's a perfect place to catch The Midnight Sun, you ask?

You can witness the phenomenon in territories where the Arctic Circle crosses. One of these territories is Helsinki!

Hot Summer Days

June, July, and August are the hot summer months in Helsinki. These are said to be the best months to visit Helsinki because the sun is out during these months. According to many travelers, you can appreciate the wonderful city during this time of the year.

Usually, the temperature doesn't go above 50 degrees during summer in Helsinki. The warmth is tolerable. Somehow, it encourages you to wander around the city with a bright mood. This is one reason why travelers flock the city during these months.

Tips on visiting Helsinki during summer:
- Be ready with raincoats for you and for your belongings; though it rarely rains, it's best to have these things handy
- Carry a bottle of water
- Wear a hat
- Wear proper attire; wear a comfortable shirt and jeans

- Wear sunglasses

Best summer activities in Helsinki:
- Attend The Midsummer Eve on June 24; it's a celebration that involves handicraft demonstrations, bonfires, folk dancing, music, spells, and a variety of games
- Attend The Taste of Helsinki; it's a culinary festival that occurs from June 16 to 19
- Check out the open-air markets
- Go on a boat tour; explore the islands
- Enjoy crayfish season; it occurs around July
- Strolling around the city streets
- Watch street performances

What's Winter Like?

Winter in Finland occurs during the months of December, January, and February. You can join other travelers who retreat to Helsinki during winter. But, take note that when you are longing for outdoor activities under the sun, winter days might not be the days for you.

In Helsinki, compared to the other parts of Finland, the winter days are notably warmer. It's rare for temperatures to drop below -4F(-20 celsius). Nevertheless, it's cold in the city. If you're inexperienced when it comes to snow, snow-covered streets and homes, and conditions below the freezing point, the place may be a shocker – unless, of course, you prepare.

Another possible shocker? During most winter days, the average day doesn't last long. After about five hours and forty-eight minutes, the sun begins to let darkness, along with cloudy weather, take charge. It can seem a bit odd for foreigners. For locals, though, it's not.

Tips on visiting Helsinki during winter:
- Be ready with rain coats (for you and for your belongings)
- Wear the proper attire; wear a sweater, a pair (and more) of thermal socks, mittens, layer of clothes, gloves, and scarf
- When traveling by car, make sure to have studded, winter tires

Best winter activities in Helsinki:
- Go dog sledding
- Go ice breaker sailing
- Go ice fishing
- Go skiing
- Ride a snowmobile
- Stay in an igloo
- Watch a local hockey match
- Watch the northern lights

4

What You Need to Know about Transportation

The Helsinki Airport: Offering Excellent Service

The Helsinki Airport (HEL) is an international airport. It's located 17 km north of the Helsinki City Center, in Vantaa. It's operator is Finnavia and it serves as a hub for different air carriers.

Helsinki Airport Website
http://www.finavia.fi/en/helsinki-airport/
Helsinki Airport Map
https://goo.gl/maps/bUgF58GRj0q

Getting Into Helsinki

You can get into Helsinki by train, bus or taxi.
Helsinki Airport Transport Website
http://www.finavia.fi/en/helsinki-airport/to-and-from/train-buses-and-taxis/
Helsinki Airport Rail Website
https://www.hsl.fi/en/timetables-and-routes/terminals/transport-links-helsinki-airport

Some air carriers in the Helsinki Airport:

- Nordic Regional Airlines
- TUlfly Nordic
- Jet Time
- Freebird Airlines
- Scandinavian Airlines
- Norwegian Air Shuttle

According to statistics, the Helsinki Airport holds an outstanding record. Annually, it serves more than 2,000,000 domestic passengers. It also serves more than 13,000,000 international passengers.

Destinations:

- Bangkok
- Beijing
- Brussels
- Cincinnati
- Dubai
- Frankfurt
- Hong Kong
- Istanbul
- London
- Mariehamn
- Moscow
- New York
- Osaka
- Paris
- St. Petersburg

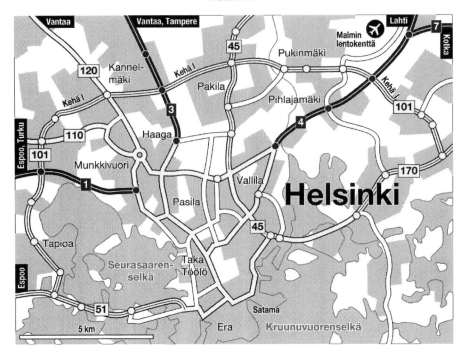

Transport in Helsinki

Helsinki Street Map
https://goo.gl/maps/a8uUZKrzMJ52

Did you know that Helsinki is Finland's only city with subways and trams?

Helsinki features The Helsinki Metro. It's a rapid transit system under the operations of HKL (or Helsinki City Transport) for HSL (or Helsinki Transport Authority). After twenty-seven years of planning, it opened to the public on August 2, 1982.

Annually, it carries an estimated 62,000,000 passengers. It has two lines (M1: Vuosaari to Matinkylä and M2: Mellunmäki to Tapiola).

Since its availability, as well as its accessibility, is impressive, why not use it as a means to navigate the city?

Helsinki Metro Website 1
http://www.hel.fi/www/hkl/en/by-metro/
Helsinki Metro Website 2
https://www.hsl.fi/en/timetables-and-routes/routemaps

Options for Getting by

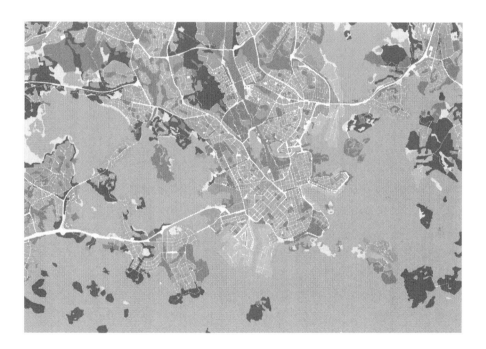

Under the HSL's management, Helsinki public transport covers transportation within Helsinki. You can now easily wander around the city and hop on to nearby regions. Among these nearby regions are

Espoo, Kerava, Kirkkonummi, Sipoo, and Vantaa.

Since it first opened in the 1980s, Helsinki public transport is responsible of 50% of commuting services within Helsinki. This suggests that more than half of the population is satisfied with the system.

Public Transport Website
http://www.hel.fi/www/hkl/en/by-tram/
Public Transport Website 2
https://www.hsl.fi/en/timetables-and-routes
Public Transport Website 3
https://www.facebook.com
/helsinginseudunliikenne

Public Transport Phone :09 4766 4000
- **Bus**

Since the buses in Helsinki are designated in chief points within the city, you're unlikely to have trouble getting around when you're sightseeing. These buses are assigned to follow many routes and most of them stop at major attractions.

A tip? Hang out at the city center; there, the buses pass by regularly. You won't have to wait long when you're searching for one, too. In most cases, less than 10 minutes is all it takes.

Bus Website
https://www.hsl.fi/en

Types of buses:

-Regional buses
-Regular buses

Route variants:
- A-variant – refers to a clockwise or lengthened route
- B-variant – refers to a counter-clockwise or shortened route
- K-variant – refers to an exception in the route
- N-variant – refers to nighttime lines (with operations between 23:30 and 1:30)
- T-variant – refers to trams to terminals
- V-variant – refers to the more direct route
- Z-variant – refers to the more direct way (along the highway)

-Trunk bus services
- **City bikes**

Another option for getting by is by going through the Banaa in Helsinki.

The Banaa is a term that refers to a lane especially for pedestrians and bicyclists. It is a 1200-km formation of bike paths. It has won the hearts of pedestrians and cyclists, as well as dog-walkers, joggers, and skateboarders.

With the Banaa and Helsinki's bike system, you can explore the different amazing points around the city by riding a bike. You also have the option to access parks, harbors, forests, and quiet fields. As of May 2016, the city features 50 bike hubs and 500 bikes that serve the city area.

Moreover, you can also avail of biking tours that private companies in Helsinki offer. It entails additional fun if you bike with a bunch of people. In fact, cycling groups aren't rare.

WHAT YOU NEED TO KNOW ABOUT TRANSPORTATION

City Bicycle Website
https://www.hsl.fi/en/citybikes
Bicycle Rental Website
http://www.bicycleanhelsinki.com/
Bicycle Map
https://goo.gl/maps/dghaGNowW9J2

- **Commuter train**

Trains are another cool way to get around Helsinki. That's according to the record of more than 800 departures on weekdays.

Commuter trains allow you to unravel the northeast and northwest regions in downtown Helsinki. It consists of 14 separate services and it runs on all the branches that start at the Helsinki Central Railway Station. Chiefly, it operates above the ground within the major areas of the city.

Helsinki Central Railway Station Map
https://goo.gl/maps/BuHLFb5xTW82

Commuter train routes:
- Line A – operates from Helsinki to Leppävaara
- Line E – operates from Helsinki to Kauklahti
- Line L – operates from Helsinki to Kirkkonummi (runs nightly and on weekday mornings)
- Line U – operates from Helsinki to Kirkkonummi (runs twice hourly)
- Line X – operates from Helsinki to Kirkkonummi
- Line Y – operates from Helsinki to Siuntio
- The Ring Rail Line – operates from Helsinki to Tikkurila
- Train D – operates from Helsinki to Riihimäki (runs as a rush hour service)

- Train K – operates from Helsinki to Kerava (runs once)
- Train N – operates from Helsinki to Kerava (runs early morning and late night)
- Train R – operates from Helsinki to Riihimäki (runs twice daily)
- Train T – operates from Helsinki to Riihimäki (runs once nightly)
- Train Z – operates from Helsinki to Lahti

Train Website
https://www.vr.fi/cs/vr/en/commuter_service_timetables
Public Transport Website
https://www.hsl.fi/en/information/how-use-public-transport

- **Ferry**

A ferryboat in Helsinki serves as another great option.

Helsinki is proud of its two ferry lines. Suomenlinnan Liikenne Oy is the operator of both lines. The ferries establish a connection to an emergency vehicle tunnel.

Two ferry lines:
- Mainland to Korkeasaari Zoo
- Mainland Soumenlinna

Moreover, due to Helsinki's location on the Baltic Sea, the Helsinki ferry port is a gateway to different European regions. Since it was founded in 1550, it continually provides transportation to countries such as Estonia, Russia, and Sweden. It has numerous ferry terminals. The trips have long sailing times of up to seventeen hours.

Ferry Website 1
http://www.hel.fi/www/helsinki/en/maps-and-transport/transport/ferry/water-transport/water-transport

Ferry Website 2
http://www.aferry.com/helsinki-ferry.htm

- **Tram**

WHAT YOU NEED TO KNOW ABOUT TRANSPORTATION

Since the 1900s, the Helsinki tram system has operated continuously. The trams run based on a network that consists of (almost) double tracks. These are powered from overhead wires.

Most of the tramways in Helsinki are situated on the street – on dedicated tram lanes. Trams have their separate traffic lights to make them distinguishable from normal streetlights. According to HELMI (or Helsinki Public Transport Signal Priority & Passenger Information), the synchronization allows buses and trams to flow smoothly.

Streetlight symbols of trams:
- Horizontal line – means prepare to stop
- Letter S – means stop
- Upward-pointing arrow – means go

Tram Website
http://www.hel.fi/www/hkl/en/by-tram/

5

HOTELS : Best Affordable & Quality Hotels

Do you want a mystical experience?

Do you want to be accommodated with uncomplicated service?
Do you want to stay in unique designer rooms?
Do you want a passionate, emotional experience with one-of-a-kind

interiors?

Do you want modern and edgy themes?

If you want all these amazing things, consider checking in at **Klaus K.**

The Klaus K

The Klaus K is Helsinki's 1st design hotel. Kalevala, the national epic, inspired its design. Since it's in the heart of the city, it provides easy access to a truckload of attractions.

Klaus K Website
http://www.klauskhotel.com/en/
Klaus K Map
https://goo.gl/maps/irCUoYBMz3p
Address
-Bulevardi 2, 00120 Helsinki, Finland
Tel:+358 20 7704700

Helsinki's Affordable & Excellent Hotel Options

Because the city was named as the World Design Capital, you can expect a wonderful time when you're in Helsinki. At almost every corner, every street, and every building you look at, you'd be swooned. Among these awesome establishments in the place are the hotels.

You don't have to worry too much about the costs. The rates are reasonable.

If you're travelling with a tight budget, you'd be delighted to know that there's a ton of excellent options for you.

Top five options:

Ava Hotel

Ava Hotel is one of Helsinki's popular hotels because of its convenient location near the city center. If you wish to spend most of your time roaming around the city, write down this hotel's name and address on your list.

<u>Star rating</u>: 3 stars
<u>Address</u>: 6 Karstulantie, Keskinen Suurpiiri
<u>Room types</u>: -Two-bedroom apartment
-Three-bedroom apartment
-Standard twin room
-Studio apartment
<u>Facilities</u>: Gym
Fitness center
Sauna
<u>Rates</u>: Around 49 € per night (for one person)
Ava Hotel Website
http://www.ava.fi/hotel-ava
Ava Hotel Map
https://goo.gl/maps/EtEJXARbSGq
<u>Tel:</u>+358 9 774751

Cumulus Kallio

Near the heart of the city is the cozy hotel, Cumulus Kallio. Once you've experience Helsinki's attractions, an extra comfortable room is waiting for you.

<u>Star rating</u>: 3 stars
<u>Address:</u> 2 Läntinen Brahenkatu, Keskinen Suurpiiri
<u>Room types</u>: -Standard single room
-Standard twin room
-Superior double room
-Superior triple room

Facilities: Bowling alley
Cycling station
Gym
Sauna
Swimming pool
Rates: Around 150 € per night (for one person)
Cumulus Kallio Website
https://www.cumulus.fi/en/hotels/cumulus-kallio-helsinki
Cumulus Kallio Map
https://goo.gl/maps/W5RDhCbq2vD2
Tel: +358 200 48109

Dommus Academia

Are you interested in staying at an eco-friendly place in Helsinki? Dommus Academia is the hotel to check into! If you don't want any trouble when hopping from the hotel to other parts of the city, you won't regret your stay. A bus and metro stations are just five minutes away from the location.

Star rating: 3 stars
Address: 14 Hietaniemenkatu, Eteläinen Suurpiiri
Room types: -Single room
-Twin room
-Triple room
-Bunk bed (male dormitory)
-Bunk bed (female dormitory)
-Economy single room
-Economy twin room
Facilities: Gift shop
Restaurant
Sauna
Rates: Around 40 € per night (for one person)
Dommus Academia Website

http://www.hostelacademica.fi/
Dommus Academia Map
https://goo.gl/maps/BtsGkoDd6R92
Tel:+358 9 13114334

Forenom Merihaka

If you start your day with a cup of coffee, the coffee maker inside your room at Forenom Merihaka will set you in a great mood when exploring Helsinki. You can then head to the nearby cathedral and music center for vibes that are more positive.'

Star rating: 2 stars
Address: 7 to 9 Haapaniemenkatu, Keskinen Suurpiiri
Room types: -Single room w/ shared bathroom
-Double room w/ shared bathroom
Rates: Around 50 € per night (for one person)
Forenom Merihaka Website
http://forenom.fi/en/hostels/helsinki-merihaka/
Forenom Merihaka Map
https://goo.gl/maps/ehtajTnTNhM2
Tel:+358 20 1983420

Omena Hotel

Because the Helsinki Central Station is just around the corner, consider Omena Hotel. It's a fine hotel for a brief stay in Helsinki. The interiors are quite basic, but they make way for a relaxing scene. Staying at this place is a great idea for two reasons: it's near the central station and the rates are reasonable.

Star rating: 3 stars
Address: 13 Lönnrotinkatu, Eteläinen Suurpiiri

Room types: –Single room
–Double room
–Family room
Rates: 49 € per night (for one person)
Omena Hotel Website
https://www.omenahotels.com/en/hotels/helsinki-lonnrotinkatu-en/
Omena Hotel Map
https://goo.gl/maps/DV5cUjF8FCM2
Tel:+358 600 555222

6

Let's Eat: Best Restaurants in Helsinki

One famous delicacy in Helsinki is **perunarieska**.

Perunaieska is potato flat bread. Its main ingredients are potatoes, barley flour, and eggs.

It became a top delicacy in Helsinki because of the harsh climate during most days of the year. The regular unavailability of fresh fruits and vegetables made the locals highly reliant on potato (among many staple tubers).

Nowadays, people in Helsinki add extra excitement to their signature flavors. Before, it was more about stable tubers. Well, long gone are those days.

Excellent Restaurants around Helsinki

All around Helsinki, finding a retreat to satisfy a hungry stomach is effortless. Along most streets are lineups of snack bars and restaurants.

As the locals would advise, if you want to try the best salivating flavors of Helsinki meals, make sure to stop by at particular restaurants. Whether you're on the lookout for Finnish delicacies or you want a dish of international favorites, the finest should be the ones worth checking out.

Top five restaurants:

- Chef & Sommelier

Looking for organic delicacies? Looking for sumptuous meals?

If so, Chef & Sommelier is the place to go. It's located within walking distance from the city center. Because of its healthy European and Scandinavian themes, it's a favorite of the locals. According to the locals, the food, along with its service, is excellence personified.

Menu includes:
Buckwheat and ransom
Cabbage and beans
Carrot and pine

Cucumber and sour milk
Lapland cow
Meadowsweet
Rhubarb and rose
Whitefish and herbs

Chef & Sommelier Website
http://chefetsommelier.fi/en/
Chef & Sommelier Map
https://goo.gl/maps/372g7itfTaK2
Phone :+358 40 0959440
Address: Huvilakatu 28, 00150 Helsinki

- Juuri

For a glorious serving of Finnish flavors and a selection of unique beers, Juuri is the restaurant to dine in. Especially if you're quite restless from city tours, the place won't disappoint. According to reviews, the setting is splendid!

Menu includes:
Grilled beef with cauliflower
Salt caramel cake
Cucumber soup
Organic egg with mushrooms
Whitefish with horseradish and elderflower
Quark with marjoram
Juuri Website
http://juuri.fi/en/
Juuri Map
https://goo.gl/maps/55mvwtvFwJs
Phone :+358 9 635732
Address: Korkeavuorenkatu 27, 00130 Helsinki

- Nokka

At Nokka, the meals are nothing short of appetizing. As the locals put it, everything in the menu is well crafted. The foods are delicious, the choice of wines is excellent, and the overall presentation is impressive.

To top it off, Nokka is situated in a fascinating setting. It's located is in a traditional building with awesome interiors. It boasts of wonderful views, as well.

Menu includes:
Rhubarb and quinces
Air-dried asparagus
Domestic cheese
Nokka Website
http://www.ravintolanokka.fi/en/front-page/
Nokka Map
https://goo.gl/maps/k4L3ibwszQ62
Phone : +358 9 61285600
Address: F, Kanavaranta 7, 00160 Helsinki

- Ragu

Ragu serves Central European, European, and Scandinavian delights to everyone in Helsinki. If you're craving for those kinds of flavors, your next destination should be at this restaurant. According to the locals, it's as if you can't admire the place enough. The foods and drinks were spectacular!

Menu includes:
Cockerel breast and liver
Organic lamb sirloin and neck
Shellfish
Pike Wallenberg with potato

Ragu Website
http://www.ragu.fi/
Ragu Map
https://goo.gl/maps/FEJsvJqhtxQ2
Phone :+358 9 596659
Address:Ludvigsgatan 3, 00130 Helsinki

- Ravintola Tokyo55

If you're hungry for sushi and other Japanese and Asian favorites, head to Ravintola Tokyo55. It has flavorful meals and cool cocktails.

Ravintola Tokyo55's location is quite far from Helsinki's city center. While some are not pleased, other people are fine with it being off the city. For those who prefer a quiet setting, it serves as the ideal place.

Menu includes:
Scampi
Miso soup
Green tea ice cream
Duck liver

Ravintola Tokyo55 Website
http://tokyo55.fi/menu/
Ravintola Tokyo55 Map
https://goo.gl/maps/U8s6VwjqC4K2
Phone :+358 9 43427640
Address:Runeberginkatu 55b, 00260 Helsinki

7

Exploring The Legendary Landmarks in Helsinki

There's this unique church in Helsinki. Its underground interior is composed of Helsinki peninsula's solid rock.

Tuomo Suomalainen and Timo Suomalainen designed it in the 1960s. It shows a shallow circular dome of glass borne and copper sheeting on concrete ribs. Its inside features a glazed dome where exquisite natural light permeates.

It attracted a string of controversies from religious sectors. A few of its nicknames before include "devil defense bunker" and "million mark church". Despite the negative side to its reputation, its popularity for musicians remains. Mainly because of its amazing acoustics, the church is used as a venue for musical events.

It's called *Helsinki's Rock Church or Temppeliaukio*. It's one of the plethora of legendary attractions in the city.

Helsinki's Rock Church Website
http://www.helsinginkirkot.fi/en/churches/rock-church-temppeliaukio
Helsinki's Rock ChurchMap
https://goo.gl/maps/yMgsKjdF4yo
Phone :+358 9 23406320
Address:Lutherinkatu 3, 00100 Helsinki

What Makes an Attraction Legendary?
There are countless landmarks all around Helsinki. While they're all important, some landmarks are a notch more fascinating. Others prefer to hop on a plane and travel hundreds, if not thousands, of miles

just to catch a glimpse.

When you're in Helsinki, maybe you should join a flock of travelers who visit a particular landmark.

Top five attractions:

(1)Kauppatori (or Market Square and Salutorget)

Kauppatori, on the harbor side, is a tourist favorite in Helsinki. Especially during spring and autumn, it's loaded with activities. You can check out different stalls as you walk around.

Most travelers usually hang out in the area. They stroll with snacks in hand. You can follow their lead, too. But, try not to be caught off guard if a seagull grabs your snack. The animal is with many others of its kind.

What to expect:

- Outdoor cafes
- Fresh fish (for sale)
- Scarves (mostly during the winter season)
- Knit hats (mostly during the winter season)
- Furs (mostly during the winter season)
- Organic products (for sale)
- Ferry cruise service
- Finnish foods (for sale)
- Finnish souvenirs (for sale)
- Exhibition of old American cars

Kauppatori Map
https://goo.gl/maps/JEsAvzYfDHQ2
Phone : +358 9 31023565
Address: Eteläranta, 00170 Helsinki

(2)The Fortress of Suomenlinna (& the island of Suomenlinna)

In the 1700s, Sweden built a fortress in the island of Suomenlinna for Russia's protection. This building is called The Fortress of Suomenlinna.

In the old days, there was nothing much to see, but a fortress. Today, the place has gone up another level. The fortress' restoration made it a thing of beauty. It became a magnificent site, and the people behind UNESCO agree. It's been named a World Heritage Site.

To visit The Fortress of Suomenlinna, purchasing a ticket for a roundtrip ferry ride is a good idea. For no more than €4, the destination is yours to explore.

What to expect:
- Finnish Castle
- Canons
- Cafes
- Residential buildings

- Restaurants
- Theaters

The Fortress of Suomenlinna Website
http://www.suomenlinna.fi/en/
The Fortress of Suomenlinna Map
https://goo.gl/maps/DAuN4dJzh1s
Phone :+358 29 5338410

(3)The Helsinki Cathedral

Especially if you're a fan of neoclassical architecture, don't miss The Helsinki Cathedral. It was built as a tribute to Finland's Grand Duke,

Tsar Nicholas the first of Russia. Its completion took twenty-two years (from 1830 to 1852).

Other times, The Helsinki Cathedral is called The Lutheran Cathedral. It resembles a Greek cross with four pieces of equilateral arms. It's a distinctive landmark in Helsinki because of its tall dome that is surrounded by smaller domes.

What to expect:
- Statue of Emperor Alexander the second (at the front façade)
- Life-size statues of Twelve Apostles (at the apex and corners)
- Russian-donated altarpiece
- Free-standing bell towers
- Cylindrical pulpit

The Helsinki Cathedral Website
http://www.helsinginkirkot.fi/en/churches/cathedral
The Helsinki Cathedral Map
https://goo.gl/maps/s3Z9aYwc1RH2
Phone :+358 9 23406120
Address:Unioninkatu 29, 00170 Helsinki

(4)Korkeasaari Elaintarha (or Helsinki Zoo)

Korkeasaari Elaintarha is the ideal place for an animal lover. It has been around since 1889! Its location is on a 22-hectare rocky island that connects the mainland with a bridge. It's Helsinki's biggest zoo and one of Finland's most popular attractions.

It's also called the Helsinki Zoo. An observation tower is available so you can check out the animals from a high point. It's open to the public all year round. You can get there via a ferry, a private car, or a bus.

What to expect (animals):

- Amur leopard
- Barbary macaques
- Eurasian brown bear
- European otters
- Guanaco
- Hamadyras baboons
- Siberian tiger
- Takin
- Turkmenian kulan
- Wild horse

Korkeasaari Elaintarha Website
http://www.korkeasaari.fi/helsinki-zoo/
Korkeasaari Elaintarha Map
https://goo.gl/maps/MhmSKtYBD272
Phone :+358 9 3101615
Address:Mustikkamaanpolku 12, 00270 Helsinki

(5)The Sibelius Monument & Park

Are you interested in stopping by at a place that features an outstanding result of a fundraising campaign?

If so, The Sibelius Monument & Park is for you!

The centerpiece of the park is the Sibelius Monument or Passio Musicae. It came to be because of a debate about abstract art – its flaws and merits. It's a sculpture created by Eila Hiltunen. It's intended to honor the famous musical composer, Jean Sibelius.

What to expect:
- The Sibelius Monument (made of welded pipes that resemble organ pipes)
- A relaxing environment

The Sibelius Monument & Park Website

http://www.eilahiltunen.net/monument.html
The Sibelius Monument & Park Map
https://goo.gl/maps/VNmEdFYRmmq
Phone :+358 9 31087041
Address:Sibeliuksen puisto, Mechelininkatu, 00250 Helsinki

8

It's Museum Time: Best Museums in Helsinki

An exhibition of a taxidermist's prized possessions is among the things that a museum in Helsinki has in store for you.

For one, would you be excited to see an African elephant (that a taxidermist worked on) at a museum lobby?

With an up close encounter, among the things that you can observe about an African elephant are:
- It has a thick body
- It has large ears
- Its nose and upper lip create a trunk
- It has four molars
- It has stocky legs
- It has a concave back

If you don't mind spotting a taxidermed elephant at a museum, you're probably set on discovering more about other animals. A perfect place for you is a museum!

A Great Reason to Visit a Museum

A trip to a museum is usually worthwhile. You can learn important information, and see exclusive items. Overall, after your trip, you end up happier.

Museums feature a variety of things. Seeing these things makes you feel good. Whether you're on your trip alone or with a group, a museum is a good place to visit.

In Helsinki, there are many brilliant museums for you to check out!

Top five museums:
(1)The Bank of Finland Museum
To find out more about the monetary economics, Helsinki's The Bank of Finland Museum has got you covered. You can see exhibitions about the operations of the bank, as well as the operations of those with an instrumental part in the Finnish society.

If you think financial matters are cryptic, esoteric, and dull, a trip to The Bank of Finland Museum will make you re-think. Because the presentations come with a fun factor, you just might walk out with loads of new knowledge and a smile!

Phone :+358 10 8312981
Address: 2 Snellmaninkatu

On display
- History of money
- Banknote art
- Bonds
- Writings about International Monetary Integration
- Monetary policy
- Mutual debt concepts
- Highlights from the Helsinki Stock Exchange
- The Bank of Finland's statistics

The Bank of Finland
http://www.rahamuseo.fi/en/
The Bank of Finland Museum Map
https://goo.gl/maps/NWvyvgBjWd22

(2)The National Museum of Finland

HELSINKI

The National Museum of Finland will show you the history of Finland from the stone age until today. The museum is located in central Helsinki.

Phone :+358 29 5336000
Address :34 Mannerheimintie

On display:
- History of Finland

The National Museum of Finland Website
http://www.kansallismuseo.fi/en/nationalmuseum
The National Museum of Finland Map
https://goo.gl/maps/YwuL7NdAp262

(3)Sederholm House

To spend time in a historical playground, the Sederholm House is the place to be! It's in a central location so finding it is almost effortless.

Since it was built back in 1757, it's a lot like your grandparents' house. A visit can trigger memories of visiting a traditional house. The building is Helsinki's oldest one, as you can observe from the interiors.

Phone :+358 9 31036630
Address:18 Aleksanterinkatu

On display

- 18th century boutique
- 18th century playground
- Puppets
- Early century clothing

Sederholm House Website
http://www.helsinginkaupunginmuseo.fi/en/julkaisut/sederholm-house/
Sederholm House Map
https://goo.gl/maps/iS8ZqifrSkA2

(4)Helsinki Civil Defense Museum

The Helsinki Civil Defense Museum privileges you with a peek at arrangements regarding the city's civil defense. There, you can view the history and present-day strategies for the promotion of security during wars.

A visit to the museum is one-of-a-kind. It's not limited to viewing items. It includes a thrilling experience with dramatic sound effects of collapsing buildings and dropping bombs.

Phone :+358 9 278 2285
Address: 16B Siltaveuorenranta

On display
- Gears for crisis situations
- Gears for protection against gas poisoning and radiation
- Bomb shelter; an exhibition of preparations during the Continuation War in the 1940s
- Safety equipment

Helsinki Civil Defense Museum Website
http://hvssy.fi/museoeng/
Helsinki Civil Defense Museum Map
https://goo.gl/maps/93Y5c7h74j32

(5) Natural History Museum

At the introduction of this chapter, a feature of the Natural History Museum is shared. Apart from an African elephant on display at the lobby, there are different collections (with up to 13, 000, 000 pieces) inside. With all the items on display, the aim is to promote environmental awareness.

Since its erection in 1913, the building continues to receive praises for its flamboyant architecture – unusually flamboyant architecture. It displays a laidback concept with a touch of Gothic style. The Russian architects, M.G. Chayko and Lev P. Chicko, deserve thanks.

Phone : +358 29 4128800
Address: 13 Pohjoinen Rautatiekatu

On display
- Animal collection
- Fossil samples
- Geological collection
- Plant collection
- Mycological collection
- Mineral collection

Natural History Museum Website
https://www.facebook.com/luonnontieteellinenmuseo
Natural History Museum Map
https://goo.gl/maps/gLnatfhftmT2

9

Appreciation for the Arts: Top 5 Art Galleries

When you're in Helsinki, a must-see is the *Ateneum.*

The Ateneum is an art museum with direct affiliations to the Finnish National Gallery. Theodore Hoijer completed it in 1887. Previously, it's the home of Helsinki University of Art and Design and Finland's Academy of Fine Arts.

Its location is on the Helsinki center – near the Helsinki Central Railway Station. When it comes to classical art, it has by far the biggest collection.

Some of the classical artworks inside are *The Aino Myth* (by Akseli Gallen-Kallela) and *The Wounded Angel* (by Hugo Simberg).

Phone :+358 29 4500401
Address:Kaivokatu 2, 00100 Helsinki

Ateneum Website
http://www.ateneum.fi/thats-how-it-used-to-be-or-was-it-thematic-tour/?lang=en
Ateneum Map
https://goo.gl/maps/nvyMu3YVJAn

What Makes Art Galleries Magical?
Art galleries are magical places. They boost your creativity, enrich your mind, and improve your emotional strength. With the loads of different art collections, your creative side gets a treat.

Because Helsinki has a handful of art galleries, your trip is going to be more worthwhile if you show up at one!

Top five art galleries:

(1)Forum Box
Forum Box, an artist-managed gallery, is a cooperative that aims to enrich the cultural life in Helsinki. It stands in a space that's formerly a cold storage room. Since its initial opening in 1999, visitors would flock to the place to check out modern art works.

Artists:

- Adel Abidin
- Emilia Ukkonon

Phone :+358 9 68550080
Address:Ruoholahdenranta 3A, 00180 Helsinki
Forum Box Website
http://www.forumbox.fi/en/home/
Forum Box Map
https://goo.gl/maps/F4Z5JPnzSrK2

(2)Galleria Ama
Situated in a very flexible space is Galleria Ama. It welcomes all sorts of artworks from Finnish artists. Its focus is on present-day artworks of many forms. The exhibits include paintings, sculptures, installation, and photography.

Artists
- Kaisaleena Halinen
- Thomas Nyqvist

Phone :+358 50 589 4969
Address:Rikhardinkatu 1, 00130 Helsinki

Galleria Ama Website
http://ama.fi/
Galleria Ama Map
https://goo.gl/maps/ywYFp91UQK52

(3) Kuntshalle

Kuntshalle is an exhibition venue for modern art, architecture, and design. Its owner is a private foundation that receives support from the city. The place is a masterpiece of its own by highlighting an exquisite sample of Nordic Classicism.

Artists:
- Niki de St. Phalle
- Eero Aarnio
- Marlene Dumas
- Andy Warhol
- Helmut Newton
- Karin Mamma Andersson

Kuntshalle Website
http://taidehalli.fi/en/taidehalli/#p39
Kuntshalle Map
https://goo.gl/maps/UHMkicTiykF2

Phone : +358 9 4542060
Address: Nervanderinkatu 3, 00100 Helsinki

(4) Galerie Anhava

Galerie Anhava is among Helsinki's foremost modern art galleries. Since its establishment in 1991, it went on to become a top-notch gallery for the international art scene. It features paintings, sculptures, photography, and video artworks.

Artists:
- Antti Laitinen
- Jorma Hautala

Phone : +358 9 669 989
Address:Fredrikinkatu, 00120

Galerie Anhava Website
http://www.anhava.com/
Galerie Anhava Map
https://goo.gl/maps/EdjFw7myJY52

(5)Sinne

Sinne is an art gallery and organization that promotes the visual art scene in Helsinki's Swedish-speaking portions. With its primary goal of nurturing future artistic talents, it features experimental sculptures, installations, and different art pieces. Because of its theme, it's an ideal hangout for the young artist who shows some potential.

Address: 16 Iso Roobertinkatu
Artists:
- Jaakko Pallasvuo
- Kimmo Modig
- Sari Palosaari

Sinne Website
http://sinne.proartibus.fi/en/frontpage/
Sinne Map
https://goo.gl/maps/8K9CtYd8KRL2

Phone:+358 45 8833716
Address:Iso Roobertinkatu 16, 00120 Helsinki

10

The Best-Tasting Coffee: Top 5 Coffee Shops

Helsinki is known for its dreamy coffee scene. First, the scene revolved around the sizes of coffee mugs and cinnamon rolls. Then, the craze proceeded to lattes, espressos, and espresso-based coffee.

Nowadays, as most baristas in Helsinki agree, the coffee scene is about quality coffee + relaxing setting. It's no longer about the kinds of coffee, the sizes of the coffee mugs, or the additions to the drink. Today, it's more on the flavor of the coffee.

Why Go to a Coffee Shop?
A reason to go to a coffee shop is to receive a boost of enthusiasm. Downing the drink would make you feel more energetic and be more alert before exploring the city's wonders. Whether it's in the morning or afternoon (or even at night), you can always have a cup.

In Helsinki, the best coffee shops are just around the corner!

Top 5 coffee shops:
Café Regatta
Café Regatta is situated in a small fishing village. Inside, it displays pans, pots, shoes, and other vintage items. It serves cinnamon buns and affordable coffee with free refills.

Phone:+358 40 0760049
Address:10 Merikannontie
Café Regatta Website
https://www.facebook.com/Cafe-Regatta-official-125305227553336/
Café Regatta Map
https://goo.gl/maps/nLvAd1rgYrp

Johan and Nystrom
Johan and Nystrom is a tall coffee shop. It features tall ceilings, bulky walls, and bright-colored cushions. Though the place can seem overwhelming, the atmosphere is cozy. Inside, you can revel at a slice (or more of cheesecake, great-tasting coffee, and chocolate.

Phone:+358 40 5203623
Address: 7 Kanavaranta
Johan and Nystrom Website

http://johanochnystrom.se/en/about-us/our-places/helsinki/
Johan and Nystrom Map
https://goo.gl/maps/wiZ6rcpjceS2

Good Life Coffee

If you ask locals where the best coffee is served, Good Life Coffee is most likely the answer that comes up. They roast their own coffee. Their specialty? Filter coffee!

Phone:+358 50 3808961
Address: 17 Kolmas Linja
Good Life Coffee Website
http://goodlifecoffee.fi/
Good Life Coffee Map
https://goo.gl/maps/AS9LvuvDxR52

La Torrefazione

With an ideal location on a shopping street, La Torrefazzione is awesome when it comes to a quick cup of coffee. Alongside coffee, it delights guests with hot chocolate, goat cheese, red pesto, and other delicious sandwiches.

Phone:+358 9 42890648
Address: 50 B Aleksanderinkatu
La Torrefazione Website
http://www.latorre.fi/en/
La Torrefazione Map
https://goo.gl/maps/myuULyK3gum

Moko

Moko is a store and coffee shop combination.Moko makes the list because the location is great, and the interior is beautiful.The coffee isn't the best in town, but the atmosphere in Moko makes it well worth the visit.

Phone:+358 10 3156156

<u>Address:</u> Perämiehenkatu 10
Moko Website
http://moko.fi/in-english/
Moko Map
https://goo.gl/maps/bskLDzoJwFH2

11

Exploring the Bars in Helsinki: Top 5 Bars

The focus of Helsinki bars is on locally brewed and imported **ales**. For centuries, it has worked, and locals are satisfied. Though the process of producing ales is rather complex, bars in Helsinki prefer to serve them.

Main reason? For them, these are flavorful beyond compare.

Is It a Good Idea to Go to a Bar?

Yes, it's a good idea to go to a bar. It's one of the best places to unwind.

Since many bartenders in Helsinki are very accommodating, you can talk about your day to someone who's all ears. While you enjoy a flavorful glass of your chosen beer, you can narrate tales and be as detailed as you wish.

If you don't have money on hand to pay for your drinks, don't fret. Most of the bars in the city accept cards. In fact, these places prefer payment via credit or debit card.

If you want to celebrate a fulfilling day around the city with a glass of beer, you can do so. In Helsinki, you have plenty of options!

Top five bars:
(1)Musta Kissa

Musta Kissa (or The Black Cat) is a bar where you can chill and discover local Helsinki culture. It's designed with 1960s and 1970s Finnish furniture. There, you can enjoy beer and engage in worthwhile conversation.

Phone:+358 40 7711785
Address:15 Toinen Iinja
Musta Kissa Website
http://www.barmustakissa.fi/
Musta Kissa Map
https://goo.gl/maps/fmpdw8uvNzm

(2)Bar Bäkkäri

Bar Bäkkäri is a venue that provides a hard rock vibe. Its walls are decorated with rock memorabilia of sorts – artworks, signed records, and tour posters. On weekends, it features live gigs.

Address:21 Pohjoinen Rautatiekatu
Bar Bäkkäri Website
http://www.bakkari.fi/
Bar Bäkkäri Map
https://goo.gl/maps/wGdVqRiCBHP2

(3)Liberty or Death

To have a taste of Finland's finest cocktails, Liberty or Death is the bar to go to. The place is quite small and it's dimly lit. Because of its intimate environment, you can relax as desired.

Phone:+358505424870
Address: 6 Erottajankatu
Liberty or Death Website

https://www.facebook.com/pages/Liberty-Or-Death/297266020341987
Liberty or Death Map
https://goo.gl/maps/MnQWzhFJ6MR2

(4)Bar Molotow

A "respectable" bar in Helsinki is Bar Molotow. The place features enjoyable indie, punk, and rock music. With a Scandinavian functionalist design as its theme, it's a happy place for many young rockers.

Phone:+358 40 1234567
Address: 29 Vaasankatu
Bar Molotow Website
https://www.facebook.com/Bar-Molotow-156875074356672/
Bar Molotow Map
https://goo.gl/maps/3H7ZbKhkrL92

(5)Siltanen

Siltanen is a bar that displays a live gig venue. It's a great place to hang out in because it offers fairly priced menus. It features local and international musicians who play tracks of different genres.

Phone:+358 44 0660530
Address: 13 B Hameentie
Siltanen Website
http://www.siltanen.org/siltanen/
Siltanen Map
https://goo.gl/maps/ZfA6JFJEJE72

12

How to Enjoy a Night in Helsinki: Top 5 Night Clubs

Spending a night out in Helsinki?

Make your night count by going to a night club! Because the locals are their own version of accommodating, it's not rare for you to meet a friend.

With beer, food, and great music, you can be as merry as desired with your new mate.

Let him share a story of his life.

Let him tell you about a friend.

Let him talk about his sentiments with you.

Let him narrate his day.

And perhaps, let him give you travel advice.

Let him be for an hour or more and you're unlikely to regret it in the morning. All the fun is possible if you visit one of the night clubs in the city!

Why Check in at a Night Club?

Like in most places, Helsinki's nightlife is fascinating. A reason to check in at one of the city's night clubs is that it's a source of pure fun at night. When most of the locals are asleep, others are too energetic not to have a splendid time.

If you want to experience the city's vibrant nightlife and be jolly until you pass out, a night club's a great place to be!

Top 5 nightclubs:
(1)Ateljee Baari

Ateljee Baari has a very edgy atmosphere that attracts the classy locals. It's a famous night club. Apart from the foods and drinks, people visit to catch a breathtaking view of the rooftops in Helsinki.

Phone:+358 9 43366340
Address:5 Kalevankatu
Ateljee Baari Website
https://www.raflaamo.fi/en/helsinki/atelje-bar
Ateljee Baari Map
https://goo.gl/maps/ay7pTiv7oTA2

(2)Nightclub Kaarle XII

A night club that houses six bars in the venue is Nightclub Karle XII. It has a nice setting that is complemented by dancing pop music. The usual crowd inside is composed of the young and the restless.

Phone:+358 20 7701470
Address:40 Kasarmikatu
Nightclub Kaarle XII Website
https://www.facebook.com/KaarleXII/

Nightclub Kaarle XII Map
https://goo.gl/maps/zFVYEwiniUr

(3)The Tavastia and Semifinal Nightclubs

The Tavastia and Semifinal Nightclubs are originally two night clubs. They've been merged to attract more audiences from Helsinki. It features wonderful live music from folks in Europe and the US.

Phone:+358 9 77467420
Address: 4 to Kekkosenkatu
The Tavastia and Semifinal Nightclubs Website
http://www.tavastiaklubi.fi/en_GB/
The Tavastia and Semifinal Nightclubs Map
https://goo.gl/maps/1mwfqZLVuP32

(4)Le Bonk

Le Bonk is a stylish club with a fantastic atmosphere.The focus of this club is not rock music; it's more of a glitz and glamor type of club.So if you are looking for something different, then this club is for you.This club has a nice terrace and is a great place to dance the night away.Sometimes Le Bonk has live music.

Phone:+358 40 5646661
Address:Yrjönkatu 24
Le Bonk Website
https://www.facebook.com/lebonkhelsinki
Le Bonk Map
https://goo.gl/maps/xFxJjG4ZdXH2

(5)Kuudes Linja

If you want to enjoy a wild night of partying and dancing with a live DJ, then go to Kuudes Linja.They play a variety of music ranging from reggae to techno.

Phone:+358 40 5397599
Address:Hämeentie 13 B
Kuudes Linja Website
https://www.facebook.com/kuudeslinja
Kuudes Linja Map
https://goo.gl/maps/mq9NGTEGUB12

13

Only in Helsinki: The Special Things that You Can Do in the City

The Töölönlahti Bay is one of Helsinki's gems. You can access it by first, heading to the city center, then walking along a circular path. Surrounding it is a number of famous establishments such as *The Parliament House, Sininen Villa, and Finlandia House.*

It's set in a relaxing environment, and it boasts of a majestic view. While it's usually a quiet retreat, joggers can sometimes crowd the bay.

A majestic site in the bay is *The Winter Gardens*. You can find it at the northern area. Since it features a plethora of plants, the place is a treat for plant-lovers.

The *Töölönlahti Bay* is just one Helsinki attraction. When walking around the city, there's more for you to explore.

Töölönlahti Bay Map
https://goo.gl/maps/nDcg9U5WXA42

Your Very Own City Tour
Don't forget that Helsinki is a hodgepodge of architecture. The establishments feature beautiful designs including *Jugend or Art Nouveau, Neoclassical, Vernacular, and Modern-Day architecture*.

Checking out the different buildings all around the city is a treat. It's as if you are learning about its personality and its history.

Thus, feel free to plan a personal city tour. Walk around, take the bus, go on board a tram, or ride a car. You don't have to do anything per se. You simply have to admire your surroundings.

Helsinki Bus Tour Website
http://www.redbuses.com/hop-on-hop-off-helsinki/

Linnanmäki Amusement Park: A Fun-Filled Destination
Hungry for a psychedelic experience in Finland's tallest roller coaster?
If so, prepare to be blown away by the *Vonkaptuous* at Linnanmäki

Amusement Park.

The Vonkaptuous is just one thrilling ride at the amusement. There are more than thirty amusement rides within the place. Among the choices are bumper cars, water and steel roller coasters, carousels, octopus rides, Ferris wheels, and galloping horse rides.

Phone:+358 10 5722200
Address:Tivolikuja 1, 00510 Helsinki
Linnanmäki Amusement Park Website
http://www.linnanmaki.fi/en
Linnanmäki Amusement Park Map
https://goo.gl/maps/s8nebfwFFJF2

Relax at Central Park

Keskuspuisto or Helsinki's central park is the place to be for a relaxing time. It's an incredibly massive park at the heart of the city. It features a manicured garden, walking trails, biking paths, and an entrance to a forest.

In the park, you can sit down for a picnic, enjoy mindless laughter with new friends or just chill. Especially if you want to take a break and view the life in Helsinki, finding a spot at central park is a great idea.

Phone:+358 9 3101673
Central Park Website
http://www.hel.fi/hel2/keskuspuisto/eng/1centralpark/
Central Park Map
https://goo.gl/maps/xXxptc3ygbx

Visit the Olympic Stadium
Helsinki's Olympic Stadium is a one-of-a-kind place. It's located at the top of a lake and to the northern area of a large hall. It's a famous venue of historical matches, and it houses a 72m tower and a museum.

To feel majestic and appreciate an amazing view of Helsinki, take a trip to the stadium.

Phone:+358 9 4366010
Address:Paavo Nurmen tie 1, 00250 Helsinki
Olympic Stadium Map
https://goo.gl/maps/WBsRJMseCk72

14

Mind Your Safety

Did you know that Helsinki is crowned as the most honest city in the world?

According to a study conducted by the team at the Readers' Digest, eleven out of twelve locals would willingly return a wallet that's not their own. Compared to locals in Mumbai (India) and Lisbon (Portugal), it's an outstanding record.

With honest locals, Helsinki seems to be a safe zone for you. Isn't it comforting to be surrounded by trustworthy folks who have their hearts on the right place?

Why Mind Your Safety?
Minding your safety while travelling brings you peace of mind. It's important to know what to expect beforehand. Doing so allows you to prepare. Because you feel secure, you become less anxious of the possibilities. Ultimately, you can enjoy your trip even more.

It's a good thing that Helsinki is reputed as one of the safest places in the world. It wouldn't hurt to keep in mind a few safety tips.

Safety tips:
Watch Out!
- Watch out for drunkards. The locals in Helsinki are quite merry and joyful. It's a good thing. But, when they've had too much to drink, they can be too much. Fortunately, an exhibition of violent behavior is rare. Stay away from them, though. They can drive you nuts!
- The sight of panhandlers and beggars isn't rare. Since they can be very persistent, you may want to avoid these people on the streets.
- A snowy day in June? In Helsinki, it isn't rare. Be ready with clothes for protection against a spontaneous cold weather.
- Borreolosis is a disease caused by mites. When hanging out at sea sides, be watchful of small animals. Mites might infest these animals.

Road Safety
- Be careful of slippery roads and tram stops. Helsinki accommo-

dates snow many days of the year. When snow melts, some places can be unsafe for mindless walking.
- Always keep your eyes on the road when driving. It's not rare for moose and white-tailed deer to cross the streets.

Roaming around
- Always pay attention to the walk signs when crossing the streets. Since they can change swiftly, they pose threats for slow pedestrians.
- When walking around the city, please stick to pedestrian crossing lanes. Some drivers have the tendency to drive extraordinarily fast.

Helsinki Emergency Numbers
General emergencies call- 112
Helsinki Emergency Website
http://www.hel.fi/www/Helsinki/en/socia-health/health/emergency

HELSINKI

15

Experiencing Helsinki: A 3-Day Travel Itinerary

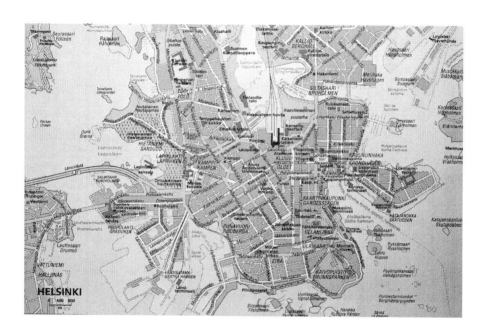

If you plan to visit Helsinki for three days, make sure to maximize your trip. After choosing a quality hotel, stop by at the finest places in Helsinki. The city in Finland is an awesome city to travel to. Let your stay be a memorable one!

A tip is to create an itinerary. Set a schedule, organize, and make priorities. Based on the information throughout this book, you have a good idea of the wonders of Helsinki.

Here's a sample 3-day itinerary. You can use it as it is, or use it and modify some parts according to preference.

Day 01
TIME
- **ACTIVITY**
- **VENUE**

7:00 AM to 8:00 AM
- Have coffee and breakfast
- Good Life Coffee

8:00 AM to 9:00 AM
- Walk around the city
- Helsinki

9:00 AM to 10:00 AM
- Visit a museum
- Natural History Museum

10 AM to 12:00 noon
- Have lunch
- Juuri

12:00 noon to 1:00 PM
- Check out a legendary attraction
- The Helsinki Cathedral

1:00 PM to 2:00 PM
- Go to an art gallery
- Gallerie Anhava

2:00 PM To 3:00 PM
- Have coffee and some snacks
- Johann and Nystrom

3:00 PM to 4:00 PM
- Visit a museum
- Helsinki Civil Defense Museum

4:00 PM to 5:00 PM
- Hang out a relaxing place
- Central Park

5:00 PM to 7:00 PM
- Have dinner
- Chef & Somelier

7:00 PM TO 8:00 PM
- Go to an art gallery
- Sinne

9:00 PM to 10:00 PM
- Have a drink at a bar
- Liberty or death

Day 02
TIME
- **ACTIVITY**
- **VENUE**

7:00 AM to 8:00 AM
- Have coffee and breakfast
- Moko Café

8:00 AM to 10:00 AM
- Check out a legendary attraction
- Korkeasaari Elaintarha

10 AM to 12:00 noon
- Have lunch
- Ragu

12:00 noon to 1:00 PM
- Visit a museum
- Sederholm House

1:00 PM to 2:00 PM
- Go to an art gallery
- Forum Box

2:00 PM To 3:00 PM
- Roam around the city
- Helsinki

3:00 PM to 4:00 PM
- Visit a museum
- The National Museum of Finland

4:00 PM to 5:00 PM
- Check out a legendary attraction
- The Sibelius Monument & Park

5:00 PM to 7:00 PM
- Have dinner
- Ravintola Tokyo55

8:00 PM to 9:00 PM
- Have a drink at a bar
- Siltannen

9:00 PM to 10:00 PM
- Have a drink at another bar
- Bar Bäkkäri

10:00 PM to 11:00 PM
- Go to a night club
- Nightclub Kaarle XII

Day 03
TIME
- **ACTIVITY**
- **VENUE**

EXPERIENCING HELSINKI: A 3-DAY TRAVEL ITINERARY

<u>7:00 AM to 8:00 AM</u>
- Have coffee and breakfast
- Café Regatta

<u>8:00 AM to 9:00 AM</u>
- Go somewhere majestic
- Olympic Stadium

<u>9:00 AM to 10:00 AM</u>
- Visit a museum
- The Bank of Finland Museum

<u>10 AM to 12:00 noon</u>
- Have lunch and buy souvenirs
- Kauppatori

<u>12:00 noon to 1:00 PM</u>
- Go somewhere majestic
- Linnanmäki Amusement Park

1:00 PM to 2:00 PM
- Go to an art gallery
- Kuntshalle

2:00 PM To 3:00 PM
- Have coffee and some snacks
- La Torrefazione

3:00 PM to 5:00 PM
- Hang out a relaxing place
- The Fortress of Suomenlinna

5:00 PM to 7:00 PM
- Have dinner
- Nokka

7:00 PM TO 8:00 PM
- Go to an art gallery
- Galleria Ama

8:00 PM to 9:00 PM
- Have a drink at a bar
- Bar Molotow

9:00 PM to 10:00 PM
- Have a drink at another bar
- Musta Kissa

10:00 PM to 11:00 PM
- Go to a night club
- Kuudes Linja

EXPERIENCING HELSINKI: A 3-DAY TRAVEL ITINERARY

16

Conclusion

I want to thank you for reading this book! I sincerely hope that you received value from it.

If you received value from this book, I want to ask you for a favour. Would you be kind enough to leave a review for this book on Amazon?

Ó Copyright 2016 by Gary Jones − All rights reserved.
This document is geared towards providing exact and reliable information in regards to the topic and issue covered. The publication is sold with the idea that the publisher is not required to render accounting, officially permitted, or otherwise, qualified services. If advice is necessary, legal or professional, a practiced individual in the profession should be ordered.

− From a Declaration of Principles which was accepted and approved equally by a Committee of the American Bar Association and a Committee of Publishers and Associations.

In no way is it legal to reproduce, duplicate, or transmit any part of this document in either electronic means or in printed format. Recording of this publication is strictly prohibited and any storage of this document is not allowed unless with written permission from

CONCLUSION

the publisher. All rights reserved.

The information provided herein is stated to be truthful and consistent, in that any liability, in terms of inattention or otherwise, by any usage or abuse of any policies, processes, or directions contained within is the solitary and utter responsibility of the recipient reader. Under no circumstances will any legal responsibility or blame be held against the publisher for any reparation, damages, or monetary loss due to the information herein, either directly or indirectly.

Respective authors own all copyrights not held by the publisher.

The information herein is offered for informational purposes solely, and is universal as so. The presentation of the information is without contract or any type of guarantee assurance.

The trademarks that are used are without any consent, and the publication of the trademark is without permission or backing by the trademark owner. All trademarks and brands within this book are for clarifying purposes only and are the owned by the owners themselves, not affiliated with this document.

Made in the USA
Middletown, DE
05 March 2017